Novels for Students, Volume 34

Project Editor: Sara Constantakis Rights Acquisition and Management: Beth Beaufore, Sara Crane, Leitha Etheridge-Sims, Barb McNeil Composition: Evi Abou-El-Seoud Manufacturing: Drew Kalasky

Imaging: John Watkins

Product Design: Pamela A. E. Galbreath, Jennifer Wahi Content Conversion: Katrina Coach Product Manager: Meggin Condino © 2010 Gale, Cengage Learning

For product information and technology assistance, contact us at **Gale Customer Support, 1-800-877-4253.**
For permission to use material from this text or product, submit all requests online at www.cengage.com/permissions.
Further permissions questions can be emailed to **permissionrequest@cengage.com** While every effort has been made to ensure the reliability of the information presented in this publication, Gale, a part of Cengage Learning, does not guarantee the accuracy of the data contained herein. Gale accepts no payment for listing; and inclusion in the publication of any organization, agency, institution, publication, service, or individual does not imply endorsement of the editors or publisher. Errors brought to the attention of the publisher and verified to the satisfaction of the publisher will be corrected in future editions.

Gale
27500 Drake Rd.
Farmington Hills, MI, 48331-3535

ISBN-13: 978-1-4144-4172-6
ISBN-10: 1-4144-4172-X
ISSN 1094-3552

This title is also available as an e-book.
ISBN-13: 978-1-4144-4950-0

ISBN-10: 1-4144-4950-X
Contact your Gale, a part of Cengage Learning sales
representative for ordering information.

Printed in the United States of America
1 2 3 4 5 6 7 14 13 12 11 10

A Handful of Dust

Evelyn Waugh 1934

Introduction

Although it is not Evelyn Waugh's most famous work, many critics consider *A Handful of Dust*, published in 1934, to be his finest novel. Written in a scathing if understated style, *A Handful of Dust* skewers the English high society of the years between the world wars. Waugh, who himself was a product of elite schools and the London social scene, had poked fun at modern society in earlier novels as well. But in *A Handful of Dust* Waugh employs satire and irony as a way of dealing with issues both more personal and more meaningful than mere social criticism. In his telling of the break-up of the marriage of Tony and Brenda Last, Waugh deals with his feelings of shame and humiliation after the collapse of his first marriage a few years before. At the same time, Waugh uses the story of Tony Last to ask broader questions about the role of tradition in English society as well as the value of the more modern and materialistic culture of the 1920s and 1930s. Waugh had converted to Catholicism shortly before he began the novel and, although there is little explicit mention of religion in the book, it is a highly moral story, exhibiting what Waugh believed to be the utter emptiness of secular, modern life.

Author Biography

Evelyn Arthur St. John Waugh was born in 1903, in London, England. His father was Arthur Waugh, a publisher and biographer, and his brother was Alec Waugh, also a novelist. Waugh attended the elite secondary school, Lancing College, where he edited the school's literary magazine, before enrolling in Hertford College at Oxford University. Not an outstanding student, Waugh tended to focus on art and his social life rather than on his studies. While still at the university, Waugh published short stories in student periodicals. After graduation, Waugh co-produced the 1924 film *The Scarlet Woman, An Ecclesiastical Melodrama*. In the years that followed Waugh struggled to settle into a career, studying art and teaching at a number of secondary schools. In his early twenties, Waugh was heavily depressed, drank far too much alcohol, and considered (and perhaps even attempted) suicide. All the while he continued an active social life in London's fashionable circles of young people, and he would mine both this world as well as that of elite schools for much of the material in his early novels.

In 1927, Waugh's life took a new turn as he fell in love with the aristocratic Evelyn Gardner, the daughter of Lord Burghclere. The family of Ms. Gardner, who became known by many friends as "she-Evelyn," was strongly opposed to Waugh's romantic interests as the two Evelyns became increasingly intimate. Waugh received a contract to write a biography of the poet and painter Dante Gabriel Rossetti that same year. Although Waugh wrote the book hurriedly, it received largely positive reviews. While finishing the Rossetti biography, Waugh began writing the manuscript for his first novel, *Decline and Fall*. The following year the Evelyns were secretly married, though the relationship would soon sour.

In 1928, *Decline and Fall*m a wickedly sharp satire of the life of the upper class, appeared to rave reviews, and Waugh's career as a novelist was promisingly launched. He also wrote numerous articles for newspapers and magazines and managed a growing public reputation. His personal life suffered, however, as he learned of his wife's infidelity. Much like the marriage of Tony and Brenda Last in *A Handful of Dust*, the Waughs' marriage crumbled when Evelyn secluded himself (in his case, to finish a novel) and his wife enjoyed the London party scene. There she fell in love with another man and told Evelyn so in a letter. Their marriage ended soon after.

In part as a reaction to his rejection by his wife, and in part fulfilling a long-held dissatisfaction with modern English life, Waugh converted to Catholicism and was received officially into the Church in 1930. From this point on, his novels would be deeply affected by his religious faith. They would also reflect his worldwide travel, often done as a journalist, which resulted in popular works of travel writing. His novels continued to be comic and satirical, often at the expense of the English elite. *A Handful of Dust*, which appeared in 1934, was no exception and also contained a scathing though disguised portrait of his marriage. When the Catholic Church annulled Waugh's first marriage in 1936, he quickly married again, this time to Laura Herbert, also a member of the English gentry. Herbert's family had converted to Catholicism and the match was ideal for the ambitious and religious Waugh. With the earnings from his novels, Waugh purchased a country estate, where he and Laura raised six children.

As the clouds of war gathered over Europe in the late 1930s, Waugh took the unpopular stand of supporting the Italian invasion of Ethiopia as well as the fascist side in the Spanish Civil War. No fascist himself, Waugh saw it as preferable to Marxism and the lesser of two evils. When England went to war against fascism in 1939, Waugh joined the Royal Marines. His experiences in battle became the basis for his highly regarded wartime novels, including *Put Out More Flags*m published in 1942, and *Brideshead Revisited*, published in 1945. It was this latter novel that would solidify Waugh's reputation in the United States, and it remains his most popular work.

After the war, Waugh settled into the life of a famous and respected novelist. He toured the United States, giving lectures. Yet the postwar American world order and the Labour government in England sickened the traditional Waugh, and he felt increasingly estranged from modern society. These feelings were reflected in his novels of the 1950s and 1960s. Seen by many as increasingly cranky and out of step, Waugh became disheartened with the democratization of England and even of the Catholic Church itself. Waugh died on April 10, 1966, after attending a Latin mass in Somerset. As biographer Calvin Lane wrote, "To the end, he remained a complex, often difficult, idiosyncratic person who could not and would not accommodate himself to the temper of contemporary British life."

Chapter 1: Du Côté de Chez Beaver

A *Handful of Dust* opens with Mrs. Beaver and her son John discussing a house fire. At first it appears they are concerned with the victims of the fire. It quickly becomes clear, however, that Mrs. Beaver's interest in the fire is financial: she wants to sell the victims' home furnishings. John, who lives with his mother, is waiting for a phone call, not from anyone in particular but rather for an invitation to lunch. Since the beginning of the "slump," what Americans call the Great Depression, he has been idle as "no one had been able to find anything for him to do." John and Mrs. Beaver discuss various members of high society and their contacts with them. Clearly, Beaver (as Waugh calls him), is peripheral to this world but labors for acceptance. He mentions that he has been invited to visit Tony Last and his wife for the weekend at their country estate, Hetton, and Mrs. Beaver advises that he reply with a telegram because it will give them no chance to back out of the invitation. The two discuss the Lasts in a somewhat critical way, though Beaver clearly intends to take advantage of their hospitality.

After Beaver receives a phone call from a lady who wants to know the name of someone Beaver knows so she can invite this other man to lunch, the scene shifts to Beaver's club, Brat's, a place at which he is not very popular. He runs into the handsome and wealthy Jock Grant-Menzies, who is a member of Parliament. They chat about the Lasts, and Jock assures Beaver that he will like Brenda Last. "I often think Tony Last's one of the happiest men I know," he continues. "He's got just enough money, loves the place, one son he's crazy about, devoted wife, not a worry in the world." Beaver checks his messages and discovers he has received a last-minute invitation to lunch. He hurriedly leaves Brat's.

Chapter 2: English Gothic-I

The chapter begins with a guidebook description of the Lasts' house, Hetton Abbey. Hetton was renovated in the 1860s in a faux-medieval style and is therefore "devoid of interest." Tony, however, loves the house and is sure it will be considered stylish again someday. It matches his boyish enthusiasm for the England of King Arthur. In fact, he names the bedrooms after characters in the Arthurian legends—Guinevere, Lancelot, and so on.

Media Adaptations

- *A Handful of Dust,* adapted as a film by Charles Sturridge and starring James Wilby, Kristin Scott Thomas, and Anjelica Huston, was released by New Line Cinema in 1988. It was nominated for an Oscar that year.

- *A Handful of Dust* was also adapted for the London stage by Mike Alfreds in 1982. The play was revived to mostly positive reviews in 2005.

Tony and Brenda seem very happy together, eating breakfast as she reads him the papers. Although Brenda seems less enthusiastic about staying in the country, their life together seems almost perfect. Outside, their son, John Andrew, rides his horse under the tutelage of Ben Hacket, who looks after the horses at Hetton. John falls from the horse but is not hurt and after more effort clears a jump. John's nanny, who is also present, is insulted by John, and she sends him to the nursery. Brenda speaks to John about this but he is disrespectful, telling her he likes Ben more than anyone else. Brenda reminds John he is a gentleman, though she later admits her scolding is a failure.

Later, Tony and Brenda receive Beaver's telegram and struggle to remember much about him. They decide to put him in the Sir Galahad bedroom because it is uncomfortable. When Beaver arrives, Tony slips off on business and Brenda entertains him. On Sunday, Tony again slips away from Beaver and enjoys his ritual visit to church. While he has little or no religious feeling, Tony enjoys listening to the reverend's sermons, although they were written and first delivered when he was overseas and bear no relation to English life. Tony also enjoys chatting after church, walking home, pausing in the hothouses for a flower for his buttonhole, and then having dinner before retiring for sherry in his library. It is a routine that pleases Tony very much.

On his return from church, Tony finds Beaver telling Brenda's fortune. Tony takes Beaver on a two-hour tour of the house, which Beaver appears to enjoy greatly. Back with his mother, Beaver admits he would like to see more of Brenda. He tells his mother that Brenda is thinking of finding a flat in

London. Mrs. Beaver is sure she could find Brenda something to her liking.

Brenda impulsively visits her sister Marjorie in London. Brenda tells of Beaver's visit. When Marjorie asks if she "fancies" Beaver, Brenda says, "Heavens, no." Later she admits she is attracted to him. They see Mrs. Beaver in a restaurant and briefly discuss a flat for Brenda. Beaver accompanies Brenda to the train station but the potentially romantic moment falls flat. The next day he telegrams her at Hetton, asking her to a party. She replies that she is "delighted." Tony notices her high spirits.

Beaver arrives at Marjorie's home to pick up Brenda for Lady Cockpurse's party. They bicker about who will pay for dinner as Beaver wonders if he should try to kiss Brenda. Both seem to have accepted the fact that they are beginning an affair. They chat excitedly at a restaurant and kiss in the taxi. As she had earlier with Tony, Brenda rubs Beaver's cheek "in the way she had." They enjoy the party. Beaver takes Brenda back to Marjorie's home. She calls him a little later but again he seems incapable of romantic talk.

The next morning Brenda tells Marjorie that the evening before was quite innocent and that she fears Beaver found her boring. She admits she finds him "as cold as a fish." When Beaver does not call her she believes their affair is over. But they run into each other at a restaurant at lunchtime and decide to see a movie. Afterward, Brenda telegrams Tony, saying she is staying with Marjorie for a few more days.

Brenda returns to Hetton and tells Tony she has been "behaving badly" and "carrying on madly with young men" while spending "heaps of money." She also tells him she has found a flat she wants in London. Tony is against it, feeling they cannot afford it and do not need it. Three days later she is back in London, where the social scene was abuzz with news of her affair with Beaver. Brenda takes the flat against her sister's advice and, once there, calls Tony. He is disappointed but sends her flowers. Beaver goes to Ireland for Christmas and Brenda is bored at Hetton. When Tony asks her if her New Year's resolution is to spend more time at home she tells him that, quite the opposite, she intends to spend more time away, perhaps enrolling in a course in economics.

Chapter 3: Hard Cheese on Tony

Jock Grant-Menzies finds Tony eating and drinking alone at Brat's. Together they get drunk while Tony unhappily talks mostly of Brenda. Brenda has Beaver call Tony, pretending to be a servant, saying she has gone to bed early. Tony calls back and tells Brenda he is coming to her flat. Brenda calls Brat's and tells Jock to keep Tony away. Jock tries to convince Tony to go to Brenda's but they end up at a seedy nightclub called 64. There Tony and Jock meet two young women named Milly and Babs who may or may not be prostitutes. Tony and Jock continue to argue about going to Brenda's, ending up at Jock's. The next day, Tony calls Brenda and apologizes for his drunken calls. She tells Beaver that all this is fortunate because Tony will now leave her alone. Tony returns to Hetton, feeling guilty. Alone, he sleeps in Brenda's room.

Brenda returns from London with Polly Cockpurse, her friend Veronica, and Mrs. Beaver. They essentially ignore Tony, insulting Hetton and talking of renovating it. Brenda talks about her flat as if she has moved there permanently. On Saturday night Brenda tells Tony she has drunk too much and cannot speak with him. The next morning she sleeps in and he goes to church alone. The next day, the women try to plan an affair for Tony. Brenda sends a woman called Jenny Abdul Akbar to Hetton, hoping she and Tony will become involved. Tony, who has no idea of the plan, greets her as a guest of Brenda, whom he expects to follow shortly. He does not like Jenny, who inexplicably calls him "Teddy." She is uncouth and pretentious and Tony is relieved when John enters. The boy speaks frankly with Jenny and later tells his nanny he thinks she is the most beautiful woman he has ever seen. Brenda arrives and encourages Jenny despite her poor start. The next morning, John finds Jenny in Galahad; he is clearly smitten with her. Jenny goes to church with Tony and he almost warms to her. Still, the scheme for romance is a complete failure. Tony is worried that their marriage is not going well but Brenda tells him not to brood. Clearly lonely, he begs Jock to extend a weekend visit. Jock cheers up Tony, which makes Brenda feel better about her treatment of him.

Jock's lover, an American named Mrs. Rattery, arrives at Hetton as the house is in preparation for an annual hunt. John begs to be as involved with the hunt as possible though the adults only want him there at the beginning. A young local woman, Miss Ripon, is also at the hunt, though she struggles with her horse. The hunt is called off and John is sent home. As they ride back to Hetton, Miss Ripon, Ben, and John are involved in an accident and John is struck by a horse's hoof. He is killed instantly. Tony sends Jock to tell Brenda and tries to make funeral arrangements. Mrs. Rattery waits behind to comfort Tony, who in turn worries about Brenda.

Tony struggles with the fact that he knows of John's death so long before Brenda. He wants to tell the extended family but also wants to wait until he knows Brenda has heard. Mrs. Rattery tries to help him forget his trouble by having Tony play silly children's games. Tony is embarrassed and the servants are scandalized. Jock arrives at Brenda's and meets Jenny Abdul Akbar. She inexplicably blames herself for John's death, claiming that wherever she goes bad things happen. Jenny then begins to feel sorry for herself. Jock and Jenny find Brenda at a party where a number of women are having their fortunes told. Alone, Jock tells Brenda that John is dead. Brenda thinks he means John Beaver and when Jock clears up the misunderstanding, Brenda says, "Oh thank God." She weeps but it is unclear that it is not from relief. Returning to Hetton, Brenda keeps to herself. She tells Tony that their life at Hetton is "over," though he does not see why. Tony talks to Jock about Brenda's puzzling behavior: she has gone off to Veronica's. There she tells Beaver that she now realizes she loves him though he seems unmoved. The following Monday, Tony receives a letter from Brenda announcing that she is not coming back to Hetton, that she loves John Beaver, and that she wants a divorce. Tony does not fully understand the letter for several days.

Chapter 4: English Gothic-II

Tony is bombarded by friends and relatives who try to make peace between the married couple. A phone call with Brenda makes Tony realize the relationship is over. In order to give Brenda a divorce, Tony decides that he will allow her to portray herself as the wronged party. His lawyer, who does not share Tony's faith in Brenda, advises him to get all agreements in writing. It is decided that Tony will pretend to have an affair and that private detectives will collect evidence against him. At first he struggles to come up with a woman to help him. Jock suggests they return to 64 and there they meet up again with Milly and Babs. The women have taken part in such arrangements before and Milly agrees to accompany Tony to Brighton, a beachside resort, if her young daughter can also come along. Tony is aghast at the idea and says no.

Tony, Milly, and the private detectives meet later at a train station. Tony is angered to see Milly's daughter, Winnie, with her, but he is unable to prevent her from coming. At the hotel, the detectives look on disapprovingly on this new twist and they tell Tony of their feelings when he joins them for a drink in the hotel bar. For his part, Tony feels that his world has suddenly become "bereft of order," so farcical are the events in his life now. Dan, a friend of Milly, arrives with his girlfriend Baby, and Tony joins them for a party.

Early the next morning, Winnie wakes Tony and demands they go to the beach. Back at the hotel, Tony eats breakfast in the dining room, only to be told by one of the detectives that they need more evidence. So Tony goes back upstairs and pretends to eat breakfast in bed with Milly. Returning from the trip, Tony meets with Reggie St. Cloud, Brenda's brother. A stout man who seems much older than he truly is, Reggie is an archaeologist and a member of the House of Lords. Reggie, who had been in Tunisia until he heard about the affair, accuses Tony of being vindictive and of pushing Brenda and Beaver together. Reggie lectures Tony about drinking too much and seeing other women. For Tony, this talk seems a continuation of his surreal life of late. Finally, Reggie demands Tony quadruple his proposed annual payment to Brenda. Tony protests that this would mean giving up Hetton and that Brenda would never want him to do that. Tony defends Brenda to Reggie but when he calls her she confirms that this is her wish. The conversation is a turning point for Tony. "A whole Gothic world had come to grief…. "His vision of his life at Hetton now shattered, Tony asserts that there will be no divorce and that he is going away.

Chapter 5: In Search of a City

The scene shifts to the deck of a ship bound for Trinidad. Tony meets a man who asks him why he is traveling. When Tony tells him he is "looking for a city," the man is a bit put off. Soon, however, Tony gains a reputation with the other passengers as an explorer. He has left England because he believes that is what a person in his circumstances should do. Tony had met Dr. Messinger, a young bearded man who tells him he is on his way to Brazil to search for a fabled city in the heart of the South American continent. Tony, who had planned to go on a simple cruise, had torn up his pamphlets and joined Dr. Messinger on his quest. In Tony's mind the city is "Gothic in character, all vanes and pinnacles, ... a transfigured Hetton.... "

Also on the ship is a young woman named Thérèe de Vitré, returning to Trinidad after years of studying in Paris in order to marry. She asks Tony about his exploring and they become friends, playing shuffleboard and other games. Nearing Barbados their relationship becomes romantic. They kiss and she asks him to visit her in Trinidad. This changes suddenly when he tells her he is married. Thérèe, a strict Catholic, is horrified and does not introduce him to her father when he greets her in Trinidad. In town, Tony sees her. She waves but does not stop to speak to him. Another passenger assures him this is typical of the local elites.

For some time during the chapter, the scene shifts back and forth between Tony's journey and events back in London. Tony and Dr. Messinger chug upstream toward "the City." Tony is tortured by the many biting insects and small animals of the jungle. Meanwhile Brenda, out dancing with Jock, says she is still fond of Tony despite his behavior. Tony camps in an Indian village, waiting for the men to return. Jock worries about the dumping of low-price pork pies on the English market. Tony hunts with the Indians and thinks of his old history teacher. Beaver admits to his mother that he does not know where his relationship with Brenda is going. Tony and Dr. Messinger walk for two weeks, speaking rarely because of their exhaustion. Mrs. Beaver suggests John should have a holiday.

Tony and Dr. Messinger's supplies run low and their Indian guides refuse to hunt because of fears of evil spirits. Dr. Messinger repeatedly asks their interpreter, Rosa, when their canoes will be ready. He cannot get a straight answer from her. Finally, she declares that the men will go no farther, though the canoes are now ready. Dr. Messinger tries to entice them with mechanical toy mice. When he demonstrates them, the Indians run away into the bush. Brenda and Beaver bicker about his intention to travel to America with his mother. The Indians desert Tony and Dr. Messinger. "The situation is grave," says Tony's companion.

Tony and Dr. Messinger travel on together, down the treacherous river. Tony develops a fever, which comes and goes, making him delirious. One afternoon he has a vision of Brenda. Dr. Messinger nurses him. He leaves in his canoe to look for a sign of a village nearby. Approaching rapids, he tries to get to the bank, but tips over, falls over a waterfall, and dies of his injuries. Brenda sees the family lawyer in the hopes of receiving more money. Instead she learns that Tony has made a new will, leaving Hetton to his cousins. Alone in the jungle and feeling unwell, Tony begins to cry. His fever returns. Brenda realizes that her affair with Beaver is over. She breaks down. Tony dreams surreal dreams, in which Rosa, Milly, Lady Cockpurse, and others discuss the widening of a road. Brenda declares her love for Beaver. Voices come and go. Finally, Tony sees a vision of "the City." It is like a gothic castle with ramparts and battlements. Tony stumbles through the jungle toward his hallucination of a shining version of the Hetton of his imagination.

Chapter 6: Du Côté de Chez Todd

Tony is rescued by a Mr. Todd, a man of European descent who has lived in the Amazon for almost sixty years. Mr. Todd humors the hallucinating Tony and gives him medicine that makes him sleep. After several days he feels much better. Tony asks Mr. Todd about his background. Todd claims to be the father of most of the people in the area. He is the most powerful man in the region but is ashamed that he cannot read. He asks Tony to read to him. Tony learns that Mr. Todd has a great fondness for the novelist Charles Dickens and has many of his books. At first Tony enjoys reading Dickens's novels to Mr. Todd, but he begins to find his host somewhat threatening. When he asks about a canoe to return downriver, Mr. Todd is evasive. Tony finds a note from an earlier visitor who seems to have shared his predicament. As Tony presses for a boat, Mr. Todd begins to hold his shotgun on his lap when they are reading. After they are visited by a prospector, Tony is cheered because he feels he may be rescued soon. Mr. Todd gives Tony a local drink that causes him to sleep for two days. When he wakes he discovers a rescue party has come and gone. Mr. Todd has let on that Tony had died. He is stuck with Mr. Todd forever.

Chapter 7: English Gothic-III

Tony's cousin, Richard Last, now runs Hetton. The staff has been reduced and life there is simpler. Over an informal breakfast with his family, he reads a letter from "Cousin Brenda." She writes to say that she cannot attend the dedication of a memorial to Tony. She is stuck in London where her new husband, Jock Grant Menzies, has business before Parliament. Later that morning, Reverend Tendril unveils a memorial to "Anthony Last of Hetton, Explorer." The novel closes with one of the Last children, twenty-two-year-old Teddy, dreaming that someday he can restore Hetton to its former glory under his cousin Tony.

Characters

Jenny Abdul Akbar

Jenny is a shallow and emotional woman in Brenda's circle of friends. Brenda sends her to Hetton to try to have an affair with Tony, but she fails. Jenny irrationally and selfishly thinks John's death is her fault because of her very presence. Despite her declarations of deep fondness for Brenda, she drifts away from her after Tony's departure leaves Brenda with little money.

Allan

Allan is Marjorie's husband, Brenda's brother-in-law. He takes a dim view of Brenda's affair with Beaver. Like Marjorie, he is "hard up and smart."

Babs

Babs is one of two young women Tony and Jock meet when they spend an evening drinking at the nightclub 64. She is surprised when the men do not go home with them.

Baby

Baby is the girlfriend of Milly's friend Dan. She meets Tony at the hotel in Brighton. She is distressed because she sees people she believes to be Jewish at the hotel.

John Beaver

Usually referred to as "Beaver" in the novel, John Beaver is a somewhat handsome but rather dull young man on the outskirts of British high society. With little money, he is compelled to live with his ambitious mother. Beaver drifts in and out of his relationship with Brenda Last with seemingly little emotion. His speech is clipped and repetitive. He seems incapable of emotion, even when he writes his lover, Brenda, a note of thanks for a lovely ring she has given him for Christmas. When it is clear that Brenda will not make him rich, Beaver goes with his mother to America, though it is fairly clear that even this was not originally his idea.

Mrs. Beaver

Mrs. Beaver is an ambitious businesswoman who uses her social contacts to further her interior design business. She appears to be without any interest besides furthering her own career and the amorous adventures of her son. It is she who pushes Beaver into the affair with Brenda Last and suggests the trip to America as a way of bringing it to an end.

Lady Polly Cockpurse

Despite her aristocratic title, Polly Cockpurse

is shallow and boorish. She convinces Brenda that Tony needs to have an affair and disastrously chooses Jenny Abdul Akbar for the job.

Dan

Dan is a friend of Milly whom she and Tony chance upon at the hotel in Brighton.

Jock Grant-Menzies

Jock is Tony's best friend and a member of Parliament. Jock is a highly eligible bachelor and had been considered a likely match for Brenda before she married Tony. Tony turns to Jock when he is confused over Brenda's decision to get a flat in London. It is also Jock who travels from Hetton to London to tell Brenda of John Andrew's death.

Ben Hacket

Ben is a worldly man who looks after the stables at Hetton. He is John Andrew Last's hero and described by Waugh as "a man of varied experience in other parts of the country."

James and Blenkinsop

Detectives hired to record Tony's pretended infidelity. They travel to Brighton where they befriend Tony despite company rules.

Brenda Last

Brenda is Tony Last's wife, a pale beauty who had been considered one of the most eligible young women on the London social scene before her marriage. She is not happy living at Hetton, finding life there secluded and boring, though at the beginning of the novel she appears to have a perfectly happy marriage. The events of the story show her to be self-centered and self-deluding as she somehow comes to see herself as the victim of Tony's poor behavior.

John Andrew Last

The only child of Brenda and Tony Last, John is a precocious and painfully honest young boy. He speaks his mind openly to guests at Hetton, often embarrassing his parents. He is interested only in horses and idolizes Ben Hacket, who looks after the Lasts' stable. John begs his parents to take part in the annual hunt. They allow him to watch and stay out of the action, but he is killed in an accident nevertheless.

Richard Last

Richard is Tony's poorer cousin who inherits Hetton after Tony alters his will. At the end of the novel, Richard is raising silver foxes at Hetton and living there with his less aristocratic family.

Teddy Last

Teddy is Richard Last's twenty-two-year-old son who lives with his parents at Hetton at novel's end. Like Tony before him, he dreams of restoring Hetton to its previous glory, though in his mind it is Tony who is the model to be imitated.

Tony Last

Tony is the somewhat pathetic hero of the novel. He is the lord of a manor house, Hetton, and wants nothing except to live there comfortably. He has never really grown up and fantasizes about the romantic past of his family and his house. He is devoted to his wife, Brenda, but is clueless about her unhappiness at Hetton. Tony is the character readers sympathize with, but his romantic nature and his blindness to the reality around him make him less than heroic.

Marjorie

Marjorie is Brenda's younger sister. She is against Brenda's affair with Beaver. She lives in a small flat in Partman Square with her husband, Allan.

Dr. Messinger

Dr. Messinger is a young, bearded explorer who leads Tony on his adventure in search of "the City." He believes he understands the Indians' minds and this overconfidence leads to his death.

Milly

Milly is one of the young women Tony and Jock meet at the club 64. When Tony struggles to think of someone to have his supposed infidelity with, he settles on Milly. They travel to Brighton but Milly insists on bringing her young daughter along for the trip.

Mrs. Rattery

The American Mrs. Rattery is Jock Grant Menzies's lover. She is an able card player and an occasional morphine user. She makes a splash by arriving at Hetton in a plane, but she fails to console Tony after John Andrew's accident.

Miss Ripon

Miss Ripon, a pretty local girl, rides a nervous horse her father hopes to sell at the hunt. She is involved in John's accident.

Rosa

Rosa is the Indian guide and interpreter hired by Tony and Dr. Messinger. She continuously demands cigarettes and often confuses and confounds the Englishmen with her statements.

Lady St. Cloud

Brenda's mother, who, although she had not initially been keen on Brenda's choice of Tony for a husband, feels her daughter's extramarital affair is foolish.

Reggie St. Cloud

Reggie St. Cloud is Brenda's heavy-set brother who returns from Tunisia to convince Tony to accept her demand that Tony give up Hetton. Reggie only succeeds in angering Tony and scuttling the divorce settlement.

Reverend Tendril

Reverend Tendril is the vicar at Tony's church. He seemed to believe he was preaching to Britons in India. The parishioners seem not to notice his references to exile from home and to Queen Victoria, who had died thirty years before.

Mr. Todd

Mr. Todd lives with the Pie-Wie Indians and saves Tony's life after the death of Dr. Messinger. He has lived in the jungle about sixty years and, unlike Dr. Messinger, is familiar with the environment and people. He claims to be the father of most of the Indians in the vicinity. Mr. Todd nurses Tony back to health but then imprisons him, demanding Tony read him the novels of Charles

Dickens.

Veronica

Veronica is a friend of Lady Cockpurse who visits Hetton and criticizes its furnishings.

Thérèe de Vitré

Tony meets this slight young woman aboard ship. She is returning to Trinidad from two years studying in Paris and is intending to find a husband. They strike up a shipboard romance but she abruptly drops Tony when she discovers he is married.

Winnie

Winnie is Milly's eight-year-old daughter who tags along on Tony's trip to Brighton. She torments Tony on the trip and creates public scenes by making him look like a monster.

The Emptiness of Modern Life

A Handful of Dust is at heart a scathing indictment of modern, consumer-oriented life. Waugh is savage in his treatment of characters, including Polly Cockpurse and Brenda Last, who seek only pleasure in life without recognizing the role of morality, discipline, and sacrifice. With the expansion of industry in the early twentieth century, the prices of many consumer goods fell sharply. At the same time, new venues of entertainment, including the radio and the cinema, opened up a world of fun for those who had the resources. And it is fun that Brenda and her group of friends seek. Waugh portrays them as shallow and lacking any true interest in each other. When Brenda's relationship with Beaver falters and Tony leaves her without much money, her group moves on in search of the new "it girl" of the season. Waugh pointedly shows that none of these characters seems to truly enjoy themselves or gain anything lasting out of their modern, urban, materialistic lifestyles.

The Folly of Self-determination

Between 1900 and the outbreak of World War II, new forms of popular culture began to promise Britons that life was what you made it. Despite this growing power of optimistic imagery from advertising, film, and other forms of rhetoric seeking to convince people they could control the outcome of their lives, Evelyn Waugh had no faith in the power of self-determination. In his mind, human beings were largely corrupt and separated from God while the modern belief that most people were mostly good was delusional. Since only God could determine the outcome of a life, people should not strive to "recreate" themselves. In fact, doing so was a form of rejection of God's design. This is clearly mirrored in *A Handful of Dust* through the plot as a whole as well in the experiences of most of the central characters. Any attempt at liberation from social bonds, such as Brenda's affair and her flat in London, or Tony's dream of recreating a gothic fantasy world, end in failure. This is also true of John Beaver's wish to be socially popular, Jenny's desire to be exotic and interesting, and Dr. Messinger's hope of becoming a scientist who understands Indians. In the end, Waugh seems to argue, people's identities are determined, and those who try to radically alter their public personas are bound to be disappointed.

Topics for Further Study

- Research the ways in which Evelyn Waugh used his own experiences, especially the collapse of his first marriage, as inspiration for *A Handful of Dust*. What did he change? How did he elaborate on his experiences and what did he do to disguise or reveal the characters of the people involved? Write a paper looking at the choices Waugh made as an author in order to use his personal suffering as a way of investigating larger ideas.

- The novels of Charles Dickens play a large role in *A Handful of Dust*. Using guides such as this one, look at the story lines of the novels Tony read to Mr. Todd. Lead a class discussion on Waugh's ambitions as a writer in the English tradition, focusing on the differences and similarities between *A Handful of Dust* and the novels of Dickens.

- Watch the 1988 film version of *A Handful of Dust* and prepare a video report for your class. Showing key scenes, discuss the ways in which the director, Charles Sturridge, adapted and perhaps condensed the novel. What did he leave out or add? Why do you suppose he made these choices? Were they successful?

- Waugh spends no effort in developing the characters in *A Handful of Dust* who are either servants or people of color. John's nanny, for example, is not even given a name. She is simply called "Nanny." Likewise, with the exception of Rosa, the people who guide Tony and Dr. Messinger are never named and hardly described, as if they were not important. Using your library and the Internet, research relations between classes and races in 1930s England and write a three-page paper showing how these prejudices are portrayed in the book.

The Uselessness of Nostalgia

History plays a central role in *A Handful of Dust*, in large part because of the rapidly changing nature of English society. Between the year of Waugh's birth and the publication of *A Handful of Dust* in 1934, England fought a devastating warm which decimated a generation of young men and crippled the nation's ability to hold on to its sprawling and expensive global empire. Thus, while the United States emerged from World War I with a booming economy and a new sense of global power, many in England came to believe that their nation's glory days were past. Many Britons took a reactionary stance against modern, socialistic England and had a nostalgic fondness for the bygone Victorian age of clear-cut social roles and expanding global power. Tony Last embodies this view, and from his introduction in the second chapter until his final hallucination in the jungle, he looks longingly back at a romanticized past, hoping somehow to be touched by its glory. Thus the names of the bedrooms at Hetton are from Arthurian legend. This is also why he prizes Hetton itself, remade in 1864, and why he enjoys the literally Victorian sermons of Reverend Tendril. Even his escape from Brenda into the jungles of South America is a search for a lost city of the past, a passageway out of the present. It is not by chance that Tony's view of "the City" is not South American but rather resembles a medieval castle. In effect, this nostalgia paralyzes Tony, making him unable to either participate in the contemporary world or to find a viable alternative to it. Waugh did not share his hero's nostalgia, however, at least not for the solidity of the Victorian age. As Tony's experience shows, for Waugh, nostalgia was another force separating people from the true nature of their lives.

Style

Irony

Waugh uses irony to create the collapsing world of the Lasts in *A Handful of Dust*. Irony as a literary style is a way authors can use words to bring out a meaning separate from the ones the actual words convey. Often, the intended meaning is the opposite of the meaning of the words, such as when Brenda writes Tony a note to tell him she loves John Beaver and signs it, "Best love from Brenda." Clearly, Waugh's intended meaning is not that Brenda is giving Tony her best love. Another example is when Waugh notes that Tony "had got into the habit of loving and trusting Brenda," the actual meaning of the sentence is that Tony is blind to the fact that his wife has been openly cheating on him. Or, to cite another example, when Brenda complains to Tony that "Everything has been so difficult," Waugh's intention is to show how selfish Brenda is, not how hard a time she has had after leaving Tony. Thus, by using irony, Waugh allows his characters to speak for themselves, to reveal their true selves through their unguarded words and feelings. This style is pleasing because it releases Waugh from having to comment on the action of the novel and keeps the narrator from hovering over every conversation. It also highlights the farcical nature of both Tony's failing marriage and the broader culture of narcissism.

The Hero's Journey

As identified by the scholar of mythology Joseph Campbell, Western literature is filled with heroes who leave home as young men, face a challenge or a danger, and return home transformed by the experience. Tony Last is clearly the hero of *A Handful of Dust*, but he far from overcomes his challenges. Like the classical hero he leaves home, though he is not altogether blameless for his situation. His journey is one into delusion rather than one of revelation. However, he is searching for the very myth that he had sustained at Hetton. Only late in his journey does he realize that "the City" does not exist. *A Handful of Dust* is in some ways a classical tragedy: Tony's fatal flaw is his inability to see the world as it is and his delusion is ultimately fatal.

Historical Context

The Great Depression

In Great Britain, the Great Depression, also known as the Great Slump, caused economic and social unrest throughout the early 1930s. Waugh makes reference to the Slump early in the novel. In the introduction of the character John Beaver, Waugh notes that since the Slump began "no one had been able to find anything for him to do." Unlike in the United States, where the economy in the 1920s boomed on a spree of speculation and credit, the British economy had struggled to recover from World War I. Throughout the 1920s exports suffered and unemployment was high. In 1926, a general strike spread from the coal mines through British industry, resulting in widespread clashes between strikers and the police. As a result of these factors as well as the crash of the American stock market in 1929, a national government was formed in 1930, comprised of representatives from the three major parties, the Liberals, Labour, and the Conservatives. Still, the economy struggled to regain its status as the world's most powerful. At the same time, England's hold on many of its colonies slipped, even as the ultra-nationalist Hitler took power in Germany (in 1933, the year before *A Handful of Dust* was published) and as Italy, led by the Italian fascist Benito Mussolini, invaded Ethiopia in 1935. At first, the government responded with measures that arguably made the Slump worse, including lowering benefits paid to unemployed workers and raising the income tax. By the mid-1930s, however, stimulating measures, such as the government-sponsored construction of millions of homes, helped the economy rebound. For those less affected by the economic downturn, the 1930s proved to be an exciting decade with the introduction of sound cinema, radios, vacuum cleaners, and washing machines. This is the world of expanded opportunities for consumerism in which Brenda and her circle move, mostly untouched by the economic downturn. By the late 1930s, preparations for war with Nazi Germany invigorated the British economy as industry retooled along military lines. Thus, the coming war, one which would again ultimately hurt the British economy, ironically helped Britain emerge from the Great Depression.

Compare & Contrast

- **1930s**: In England and the United States, a married person who seeks a divorce is compelled to prove unreasonable behavior on the part of their spouse and then wait a lengthy period for the government to finalize the divorce. When couples share a desire to end an unhappy marriage in which there has been no abuse or infidelity, they are often compelled to fabricate an affair, such as Tony Last does in *A Handful of Dust*.

Today: Although the United States began adopting so-called "no fault" divorce laws in the 1960s, the United Kingdom continues to offer only "fault divorce." Briefly, in the 1990s, reform advocates managed to pass legislation introducing a law under which couples could quickly end marriages, but it was rejected by the government. Today, it continues to take between two and five years to obtain a divorce in Great Britain.

- **1930s**: With no national system of roads and highways, travel by automobile between cities and towns was time-consuming and often frustrating. Most travel of more than a few miles was conducted by rail or, often in the case of freight, canals. In the late 1930s, a few years after the publication of *A Handful of Dust* the Ministry of Transport began a centrally planned Motorway system. This plan was shelved, however, because of World War II.

Today: Great Britain is crisscrossed by a national Motorway system. Beginning with the opening of the Preston Bypass in the late 1950s, the Motorways were a response to the increasing popularity of automobile travel. Today, 2,200 miles of motorway serve some 28 million British cars. Train travel remains popular as well. Although travel by rail lost popularity between World War II and the 1980s, it has almost regained its highest historical levels of ridership.

- **1930s**: Great Britain continues to hold on to a number of Central and South American colonies, including British Honduras, British Guiana, the Faulkland Islands, Jamaica, the Bahamas, and Trinidad and Tobago. British control of the Caribbean is especially extensive. It is through many of these colonies that Tony travels on his quest for "the City."

Today: Except for the Faulkland Islands, over which the United Kingdom fought a war with Argentina in the 1980s, all British colonies in South America have been granted independence or, in the case of the Mosquito Coast, have become divided up among neighboring countries. A handful of Caribbean islands remain under British control, including Turks and Caicos, Montserrat, and the British Virgin Islands.

English Fascism

As capitalism suffered during the Great Slump, a new political movement appeared in England, one which attracted many among the aristocracy. Founded by Sir Oswald Mosley in the early 1930s, the British Union of Fascists (BUF) was an authoritarian party on the political far right. Mosley, who had formerly represented first the Conservative Party and then the Labour Party as a member of Parliament, formed the group after a visit to fascist-ruled Italy in 1932. The BUF was completely top-down in structure, with Mosley himself the unquestioned leader of the movement. It is difficult to know how many members the BUF actually had, but the success of fascism in Italy and, after 1933, in Germany, caused many to take it more seriously than its actual size might have deserved. Still, the BUF staged several impressive mass rallies that resembled Nazi rallies in their use of spectacle. After Hitler's rise to power, Mosley also became more openly anti-Semitic, claiming Jews in Britain were all essentially foreigners and should be viewed with suspicion. He also called for increased royal power and a concentration of industry in a high commission, run by a prime minister to be appointed by the king. Eventually, Mosley would be incarcerated for the duration of World War II, and the fascist movement in Britain would collapse.

However, in the 1930s, many aristocrats and conservative intellectuals, including Evelyn Waugh and some notable heads of British corporations, were sympathetic to Franco in Spain, Mussolini in Italy, or, as in the case of King Edward VIII himself, Hitler in Germany. In fact, some historians have argued that Edward's wife, the American Wallace Simpson, in fact passed important secrets to the Nazis. Evelyn Waugh was friendly with Mosley and his wife, Diana Mitford Guinness Mosley. In fact, in 1930 Waugh dedicated his novel, *Vile Bodies*, to her. Waugh's feelings about fascism were complex. His approval of the Mussolini regime in Italy was colored in large part by his desire to support the policy of the Catholic Church. Initially, many English Catholics perceived Mussolini as a protector against Hitler's threat to Catholics, especially in Austria. Waugh's fondness changed in the late 1930s when Mussolini aligned himself with Hitler and began his own racist policies. For most Britons sympathetic to fascism, any positive feeling was snuffed out when war broke out in 1939.

Critical Overview

When *A Handful of Dust* appeared in 1934, Evelyn Waugh was already a writer well known for his satirical novels about the upper classes. Some reviewers saw *A Handful of Dust* as a continuation of this trend, though others perceived it to be more openly religious in tone. According to biographer Christopher Sykes, "When the book came out in 1934 the general opinion of Evelyn's public and critics was that he had written his best book to date." The Catholic periodical *The Tablet,* however, published a highly critical review, arguing that the book failed to represent Catholic ideals. Over time, however, it has come to be regarded as Waugh's finest work. Writing in the 1950s, the renowned critic Northrup Frye elevates Tony Last's plight to classical terms, calling it "close to a parody of tragic irony." In recent decades, critics have almost unanimously favored *A Handful of Dust* over Waugh's most famous work, *Brideshead Revisited.* Writing in the early 1990s, Frederick L. Beaty applauds Waugh's ability to simultaneously parody both the materialistic characters like Mrs. Beaver and Brenda Last as well as the powerless romantic Tony Last. "Indeed Waugh's outstanding success as an ironist in *A Handful of Dust* owes much to his ability to challenge the assumptions of both commercial and chivalric codes." Beaty points out that the novel does not preach. Rather, it argues through negative examples. "By showing the disorder wrought through living according to either instinct or hollow tradition, the novel demonstrates … the need for something higher than man-made ideals." David Wykes, in his 1999 book, *Evelyn Waugh: A literary Life,* summarizes the enthusiasm of most current critics of Waugh's work when he calls *A Handful of Dust* "Waugh's greatest single achievement."

What Do I Read Next?

- D. J. Taylor's *Bright Young People: The Lost Generation of London's Jazz Age,* published in 2009, is a history of the social circle Evelyn Waugh cavorted with in 1920s London. Full of anecdotes and gossip about the "Bright Young Things," this book offers ample historical background to the action of *A Handful of Dust.*

- *Vile Bodies,* published in 1930, is Evelyn Waugh's second novel and, like *A Handful of Dust,* it parodies upper-class customs. In this case, the setting is the 1910s, on the eve of World War I. Like *A Handful of Dust, Vile Bodies* has a dramatic change of setting and tone in the second half of the novel as the hero, Adam Fenwick-Symes, is thrust into the war.

- *Brideshead Revisited,* which was published in 1945, is Waugh's most famous novel. It is much more overtly religious than *A Handful of Dust* and focuses much more squarely on the attraction of Catholicism to Britons in the years between the wars. It is also much more nostalgic, in large part because of the disruptions of life in Britain caused by World War II. It is *Brideshead Revisited,* and not the earlier, comedic novels, which made Waugh a literary figure in the United States.

- Novelist Graham Greene was a good friend of Evelyn Waugh's in large part because both men were converts to Catholicism. In 1951, Greene published his own novel on infidelity and religion, *The End of the Affair.*

- Zora Neale Hurston's novel, *Their Eyes Were Watching God,* published in 1937, is the story of a poor African-American's three marriages in the U.S. South of the early twentieth century. The main character, Janie Crawford, is a fascinating contrast to Brenda Last and provides insight into how race and class affect people's ideas about marriage and love.

Sources

Beaty, Frederick L., "A Handful of Dust," in *The Ironic World of Evelyn Waugh: A Study of Eight Novels,* Northern Illinois University Press, 1992, pp. 86, 90, 110.

Frye, Northrup, "Historical Criticism: History of Modes," in *The Ironic World of Evelyn Waugh: A Study of Eight Novels,* edited by Frederick L. Beaty, Northern Illinois University Press, 1992, pp. 86-87; originally published in *Anatomy of Criticism,* Princeton University Press, 1957, p. 48.

Lane, Calvin W., "Chapter 1: The Artist and His World," in *Evelyn Waugh,* Twayne's English Author Series, No. 301, Twayne Publishers, 1981, p. 42.

Oldmeadow, Ernest, Review of *A Handful of Dust,* in *Evelyn Waugh: A Biography,* by Christopher Sykes, Little Brown and Co., 1975, pp. 140-41; originally published in *The Tablet,* September 8, 1934.

Patey, Douglas Lane, "Political Decade I (1930-1935)," in *The Life of Evelyn Waugh: A Critical Biography,* Blackwell Publishers, 1998, pp. 119, 123.

Sykes, Christopher, "1932-1934," in *Evelyn Waugh: A Biography,* Little, Brown, and Co., 1975, p. 140.

Waugh, Evelyn, *A Handful of Dust,* Back Bay Books, 1999 (1934).

Wykes, David, "Introduction," and "1930-1939," in *Evelyn Waugh: A Literary Life,* St. Martin's Press, 1999, pp. 8, 9, 103.

Further Reading

Kennedy, Dane, *Britain and Empire: 1880-1945,* Longman, 2002.

> This survey of British imperial history is a great introduction to the ways in which the empire affected people in the colonies as well as in Britain itself.

Lovell, Mary S., *The Sisters: The Saga of the Mitford Family,* W.W. Norton and Co., 2003.

> This history of the glamorous and scandalous Mitford sisters sheds light on the world in which Evelyn Waugh lived. Nancy was a friend of Waugh and a novelist; Unity was a close friend of Hitler; Diana was the wife of the leader of the British fascists.

Orwell, George, *The Road to Wigan Pier,* Mariner Books, 1972.

> Originally appearing in 1937, this book is one-half a report on the miserable conditions of the English working class during the Great Depression, and one-half an essay on the role of socialism in making conditions better.

Waugh, Alexander, *Fathers and Sons: The*

Biography of a Family, Anchor, 2008.

The grandson of Evelyn Waugh traces four generations of tension between fathers and sons in his famous family. Beginning with his great-grandfather, the publisher and critic Arthur Waugh, this book looks at the lives of the often unhappy, yet undeniably brilliant men of the Waugh family.

Lightning Source UK Ltd.
Milton Keynes UK
UKHW02f0828310118
317120UK00008B/352/P